Bird of the Present Moment

Paméla Overeynder

Plain View Press
P. O. 42255
Austin, TX 78704

plainviewpress.net
sbright1@austin.rr.com
1-512 441 2452

Copyright Paméla Overeynder, 2005.
All rights reserved.
ISBN: 1-891386-44-1
Library of Congress Number: 2005903961

Cover art by Karen Marie Cross

Contents

Rivers and Dreams   7

    Three Cormorants   9
    In the Clearing   10
    Rivers   11
    Invisible Threads   12
    It Could Have Been Any Day   13
    Swimming Hole   14
    Goose Bumps   16
    Footbridge   17

Bird of the Present Moment   19

    Windgrasses   21
    Bird Island   22
    Fall Comes Gently   24
    Bright Winter Sky   25
    Happy Feet   26
    Bird of the Present Moment   27

The Necessity That Calls Me   29

    Snow Geese   31
    Gratitude   32
    The Land of Happiness   33
    Mountain   34
    Sunrise   35
    More Moon than Sun   36
    Fawn   37
    Winter Storm   38
    Windswept Oaks   39
    Fragrance of Kindness   40
    Spring Arrived   41
    Patch of Grass   42
    Last Sunset   43
    The Necessity that Calls Me   44

This World Is Enough   45

    Rain Lilies   47
    Robins   48
    Branches   49
    Spring Shoots   50
    Field of Bluebonnets   52
    High Tide   53
    The Night's Meaning   54
    Grasshopper   55
    Vertebrae   56
    Blades of Grass   57
    Wading in Bear Lake   58
    Watermelon   59
    Tree Offering   60
    Hillside Theater   61
    Old Barn   62
    Migrations   63

Mind of Love   65

    Walking Stick   67
    Baby Praying Mantis   68
    Wasp   69
    Bird Being   70
    Sky of Mind   71
    Blooming Beyond Death   72
    Compassion   73
    Hammock   74
    Happiness   75
    Big Sky   76
    Night Blooming Cereus   77

    About the Author   79

For Patricia

Boundless!

"Oh world, how could I hold thee more dear?"

– Edna St. Vincent Milay

Rivers and Dreams

Three Cormorants

Just at the point between day and night
the black horse stands upright,
tall as any mountain, stands
between the new moon and me,
wild mane blowing in the breeze.

Just then, three cormorants fly
across rose-streaked sky.
Heading south
they pass beneath the moon,
and for a moment's time,
birds and moon lie cradled
in the generous sway
of the horse's back.

How I would love
to swing myself up
on the great horse's back
and fly, and fly
into the vast and starry night.
O how this longing leads me…

In the Clearing

As we stand in the clearing, talking softly,
little blue stem grasses tickling our ankles,
I see us all lying down together, as deer do,
nestling into each other, peaceful and secure,
sleeping as one body, breaths mingling,
permeated by darkness, multitude of stars overhead.

As we sleep, dreams enter each of us
through our pores, nostrils, parted lips –
and our lips smile, and we breathe as one.
Our breath takes the dreams and the smiles
and mingles them in the cool night air.
They circle the clearing, sail off through the trees
across the valley to land on the faces of countless beings.
These beings awaken from our dreams refreshed and strengthened,
with joy in their hearts and liberation on their lips.

While we sleep, some deer come close,
gaze at our sweet repose,
and knowing us as kin, lie down beside us,
their breaths mingling with ours,
their dreams folding into our dreams.
We lie together – people and deer –
permeated by salve of darkness
until we are one body, one breath, one dream.

When we awake, the deer are gone,
leaving only the matted grass,
still warm with the weight of their bodies.

Rivers

Free days I come to the river
to calm myself, to remember, to let go –
the Blanco, the Guadalupe, the Pedernales,
water, lunch, journal,
heart, lungs, feet.

I come full of ideas about the water, about the day.
If I'm lucky, they fall from my pockets
like loose change as I walk toward the water.
Other days they come with me to the water's edge.
Once I plunge in, they pop quickly to the surface
and float away– happy to be free.

After that I belong to the water –
cool or warm, muddy or clear, still or flowing.
I belong as much to the sky, frogs and birds,
the cypress branches, the stillness of the great blue heron,
to the glorious sun and to the shadows
of each tiny thing.

Invisible Threads

Near dark, I go down to Barton Creek.
The water is flowing, crisp and cold
over the sparkling rocks.

Darkness is coming down into the trees.
The last leaves – orange and yellow – stand
bright against the lighted wall of rock.

Cold earthen smells dig into my nostrils.
I shiver and stuff my hands in pockets.
A small gray cat, nearly invisible in the shadows,
rubs against my leg, longing for touch.

Great Horned Owl calls
hoo, hoo-oo, hoo, hoo. Her sound
crosses the silence, travels to me
along the invisible thread connecting
each thing to every other.
I am filled with a deep satisfaction –
a feeling of belonging to life.
As darkness thickens
a holy mist settles into the trees –
a mist made of the invisible threads
of belonging, each thing to every other.

It Could Have Been Any Day

It could have been any day –
but it is this day.

It could have been any sitting rock –
but it is this rock.

It could have been any blue sky –
but it is this blue sky.

It could have been any crystal clear water rushing over any rocks,
flushing, swirling, rejoicing in its passage,
any yellow leaf, twisting and twirling
for immeasurable moments through
the blue emptiness till it cascades into the rapids,

but it is this yellow leaf on this exact day,
this blue sky, this rock, this water,
this yellow leaf sailing swiftly to freedom.

Swimming Hole

Late afternoon – two old friends walk to the creek,
through the trees, down the rocky path
to the place where cool comes up from the bottoms
to greet our heat-filled bodies.

Before long, we slide into the cold water,
swim up to the little falls, float back down on our backs,
watching dragonflies fill the air above us –
updraft, downdraft, quick as wind.
We giggle and splash like the children we are,
buoyant and awed by the water, the quiet smells
of cottonwoods leaning out over the creek,
the last birdsong, and slowly, slowly the light begins to fade.

But we are not ready, not willing to leave this paradise.
Now we float downstream – more rapids,
more shrieks and giggles as we cling
to boulders – to each other –
watching the water whirl and flow around us.
"My arm made that," you say, as the creek
cascades around your shoulder and down your arm.

Now we pull our bodies across the rapids.
The water is heavy as lead and we are paper boats
carried again and again downstream, merry and light,
until finally our sides hurt from the laughter.
Still we don't stop until we are back in the calm pool –
at home in this summer pool.

The light is fading fast. Something calls to us,
'stay, stay,' and its reflection in us wants to stay
we feel so at ease in the darkening waters' embrace.
We stay a bit longer, comfortable as any fish,
burdens and plans forgotten,
minds flushed of every irrelevance,
bodies, water, and darkness sharing a forever secret.

We stay long past reason,
until the fireflies among the trees whisper our names.
Our hearts hang back even as we pull our bodies
from the creamy water,
even as we follow the golden, flickering lights
through the darkening trees and home.

Footbridge

Spans of time, spans of water – time builds bridges,
feet cross over, hearts long to return to the Family of Beings.

We amble out to the middle of the bridge just before dusk
on a warm summer's eve, stopping now and then to enjoy
bits of life unfolding – two older men sit on a bench,
shoulder touching shoulder, one playing the flute quietly –
old friends comfortable in their belonging together.

Young children – a girl and two boys –
play with the small bridge lights, hands on and off,
dimming and brightening, playing with the power to create.
One boy gathers the leaves of a vine near our bench.
He looks back to see if we will scold him. We smile.
After several trips, his hands full of leaves, we inquire gently,
"How many do you need?" He stops picking the leaves,
and explains how they change the color of the light.
We marvel at our own childhood
through these children experimenting with life.

I want to promise them the world will always
be this beautiful, this safe…

Life is beginning to take its place on this brand new footbridge.
Small bushes and flowering plants are growing in the planter boxes.
A man plays his harmonica, soft as breath and sweet, too.
A young woman holds her guitar like a precious child in her arms,
strums ever so softly, accompanying the song of the night:
crickets, frogs and children's voices.

Slowly and surely this night is arriving – full of itself –
sliver of new moon low in the western sky, Venus below the moon,
clouds gathering for an evening rain shower, cool breeze off the lake.
We sit on the bench, eyes bathed in lake water long after the boy
stops taking the vine leaves, and the musicians have stood up,
stretched, and walked away; until the deep line of blood on the horizon
disappears and the last of the light fades. Maybe

God has placed her hand over the sun, just for a moment,
and night is a game children play like hide and seek
until their parents call them home to the old prayer.
Now I lay me down to sleep, I pray the Lord my soul to keep....

Goose Bumps

The sun comes up again this morning,
pours in the window and hovers on my sleeping face.
I was dreaming of the snow geese.
We wake up and cook our favorite dishes.

Later we drive to the old stone house,
sit at the long wooden table facing the pond
and share our food with friends.
Outside, in the biting cold, snowflakes fall
into the pond where beaver swims on her back
while geese circle and honk –
their sounds more filling than dessert.

Someone opens the door and invites the geese inside.
They come for a moment with their rich, humid voices
and fluttering wings and the room is warm as cobbler.
Everyone gets goose bumps that go away
when the door reopens and the geese fly out.

With the geese gone, the room seems empty.
A single feather floats across the table,
lands in my outstretched hand.
I hold it up, breathe into it and watch
it float about the room. Suddenly

the room is alive again. Everyone is happy.
Even though we are already full,
we eat dessert. It is plum cobbler.
As I take my last bite,
the feather lands
on my empty plate.

Bird of the Present Moment

Windgrasses

The sun, gentle in its final descent,
casts its last glance on these windgrasses
now sheathed in golden light,
running east – whoosh......whoosh......whoosh
in great waves, one upon the other.

Each grass part of every other grass –
Long rolling sighs in great waves
rolling one upon the other,
remembering themselves
as ocean wave.

Grass not separate from wind.
Wind not different from grass.
Energy breaking loose and running with itself,
flowing nowhere in great waves, one upon the other,
remembering, remembering.

Bird Island

The trees are full of egrets.
Their long, sleek, white necks stretch and peer into the darkness.
As our kayaks approach the island
they rise up by the hundreds
squawking fiercely,
measuring and questioning.
They circle and fall back into the branches
like heavy, wet snow.
Then hundreds more rise up
on the question of the moment.
Up into the shadowy darkness.
I feel a strange thrill along my spine
seeing their white bodies
sharp against the darkness,
hearing their wild cries for solitude,
smelling their avian smells.

Their sweet, sick smell
seeps into my animal brain, unregistered,
makes my stomach feel a little queasy.
We paddle to shore.
Minutes later,
your brain hemorrhages.
Your precious blood leaks out of its vessel
and into the shadowy darkness of your brain
on the question of the moment.

We don't know what is happening.
We forget the birds, forget everything
as your undigested food comes spewing up,
as your body shudders and shakes,
proclaiming something profound.

Now you lie perfectly still,
wired to strange monitors
marking time with their beeping periodicity.
Doctors and nurses come and go.

Gurneys and gowns, tests, then more tests,
hours pass slowly.
I sit in stillness beside you
waiting for answers,
waiting for life to start up again.

What slowly seeps into us both during this longest night
and the days that follow,
is the irreducible and indestructible truth
that the present moment
is all the life we have.

Slowly, we wake up together in the Land of Happiness.

Fall Comes Gently

Fall comes gently among the wild roses
and yellow flowers in their sunny meadow.
Today I spot the first Turk's-cap berry – brilliant red.
A few yellow leaves are still roosting in the trees.
A patch of blue sky slips through the branches.

I go out to greet these jewels on faithful feet.
Planted in the soil of each moment,
they don't look forward or back.
Happiness is only Now!

Bright Winter Sky

From my desk I see a flock of pigeons.
Their dark shadows crisscross the ground
as they release themselves all at once
to the perfect blue sky. They fly out.
Moments later they return.
They launch again and again.
Who knows where they go
and for what purpose.

After the exodus a single sparrow lights
on the rose branch next to my window,
calling out a song about the sunshine –
how it warms her feathered body.
A song of the moment.

Happy Feet

Right now I am walking nowhere.
My bare feet are happy to be free,
walking on sun-warmed grasses.
Above, the wind is blowing through the treetops.
Beneath, it is blowing through my hair.
Treetops and hair are mingling in the wind.
Walking beneath the towering pines,
time passes away.

Bird of the Present Moment

As we stand and watch the sun's daily ritual –
golden clouds against a bright torquoise sky –
a very large bird, a whooping crane, I think,
creates itself from the materials at hand –
softness of cloud and infusion of light,
wings gray and belly golden, rimmed rose-petal pink.

Meanwhile the moon is quietly rising in the east.

She is all wing with a sleek, tubular neck stretched out long,
towards the north.
Her wings a blur of flapping,
yet she stays put in front of us –
bird of the present moment.
All the way home she is right there,
spread out low across the western sky.

Later, in the night, the cat gets a small, gray bird,
brings it in the house.
One wing is damaged. It can't fly.
We wake up, wipe the sleep from our eyes,
take the little bird outside,
lay it on the ground,
talk softly to it,
watch its fear and suffering,
the good wing flapping wildly.
We long to lift it high into the trees
into its nest, into safety,
know we can only pray.

Meanwhile, all through the night, the full moon
pours her light into the little bird
as we sleep and dream of whooping cranes
upholding the sky.

The Necessity That Calls Me

Snow Geese

Rosy dawn draws me up from the warm bedcovers.
I put on hat, gloves and goose down vest.
My feet walk the worn path to the pond
through a stream of silence, the kind that exists
before you first speak in the morning.
The kind of silence that comes when you
realize kindness is pure language.

I'm almost to the pond when the geese rise up.
The sound of their powerful wings
lifting off the water pierces through me.
Out of the early silence – the silence that bears kindness –
the attenuated sound of hundreds of wings
beating like so many hearts fluttering,
binds my full attention. I submit completely.

Hundreds of geese lift off the pond –
whoosh up into the new day –
the hard lick of muscular wing pumping air,
their throaty fluency filled with intention.
Soon I see long, dark ribbons tangling and untangling themselves
until the familiar pattern forms, and a leader emerges.
They circle the pond once, fly across plowed oat fields
towards a neighbor's pond, encouraging each other
with their peculiar sounds – a language my heart understands.

Joining this soundstream I am lifted
into a pastel world of pale blue sky and winter grain fields.
At an earlier age I might have envied the geese
the certainty of their path or the support of their peers.
Older now, I feel more like them –
guided by some age-old knowledge
of an ancient flyway ribboned by my ancestors
who even now are honking encouragement
in a soundstream of blessing.

Gratitude

In this time we come to know
the meaning of gratitude – for we are alive –
alive and breathing and loving life.
Suffering is understood again
and liberated from its dark and silent cave.

Alive and breathing and loving life,
we yield to things as they are.
The wheel of life turns ceaselessly
despite unspeakable loss and grief.

Simply, the sun comes up each morning
all orange and round and warm, falls
without discrimination on every face,
encouraging the heart determined to persist,
and more, to thrive.

The Land of Happiness

I wake up this morning in the land of happiness.
Sitting in the dark, beneath the Buddha's gaze
following my breath, I'm happy.
Eating breakfast slowly and mindfully, I'm happy.
Going out into the season's first cold air, happy.
Walking through the yellowing trees, happy.
All morning I move about
immersed in the land of happiness.

Later…....my mind allows one small thing
and then another to chip away at my joy

    until I catch it like a little silver fish
    on the hook of my awareness.

The river is always flowing.
Sometimes we are the fish, sometimes the hook,
and sometimes, without asking,
the pure water of happiness.

Mountain

O beautiful mountain
settling, settling down to sleep.
Your purple peaks bowing,
bowing down, down into the
gray-green creases, into
the deepening green of trees.

Your noble black, plum-stained peaks,
offset by the last light and palest blue sky,
offer transit for some mauve-colored clouds –
darkening and   m o v i n g   s l o w l y,   s l o w l y
across your spine and to the north.

The darkness comes as virgin silence,
a r r i v i n g   s l o w l y
as I sit here on the hillside,
and for long, long breaths,
I am so filled I want nothing.
Nothing at all.

As I sit here absorbed in your presence,
I feel as if some invisible being
is watching over me and blessing me.

O wondrous mountain,
what hidden messenger
lives inside your numinous, undisclosed,
unspeakable, awe-full country –
a country with the power
to take away my want
and for   l o n g   m o m e n t s ...
to grant me eternity,
calmly abiding.

Sunrise

Slowly, slowly the darkness is leaving.
A faint light swells and lifts
until a shape emerges, takes the darkness,
as the sun crowns through
the cervix of NOW.
Such simple eloquence.
Such precision of purpose.

I step into the day's new light.
Deep easterly slant falls golden
across hills and over draws,
burning its way up from the other side,
lighting trees and grasses
and the wings of birds as it goes.

Every sunrise is pure silence.
Hearing the sound inside the silence,
our bodies tremble and hum
but we cannot speak of it.
Only feel the honeyed arms of its sweet ascent
sheathing us in its certitude,
only surrender to its pilgrim need.

I step into the golden, fruited,
and slender fingers of light
glazing me with their warmth,
my hands raised in greeting.
My face imitates the sun's round glowing.
My body becomes a vessel for its soundless sound
as my heart crowns through the cervix of NOW.
Quiet like the sunrise.

More Moon than Sun

The sun is floating away –
poised between two poplars –
suspended in stillness
just above the horizon.

A lush plum –
more moon than sun,
more God than God.
Slowly, slowly sinking

towards that porous line
between day and night,
passing through layers of cloud
from deepest plum to palest wisp.

Like this it slips away –
part of the great miraculous!
A lush plum –
more moon than sun,
more God than God.

Fawn

Quick as brush of cheek
she flew before my eyes
wilder than wild.

She saw me first, then
leaped across the woodpile,
her body perfectly arched.

Lithe as a willow,
faster than thought,
she flew before my eyes

leaving a blur of spots
and elegant need
in the center of me.

Leaving a blur of spots
and elegant need
in the center of me.

Winter Storm

The sky quickens and grows unnaturally dark.
There's a moment of absolute stillness. Then the light changes
and everything is suddenly glowing three shades brighter.
All activity stops. The shiny black beetle stops trudging along.
The birds clam up. No leaf stirs. The grasses are still.
Children grow quiet. Then comes a whistling sound
as cold air hits warm, electrifying
this time of momentary incoherence.
What an exquisitely alive moment this is!
I throw myself into the whirlwind of falling yellow leaves.
Every hair on my body stands on end
as I blend with the air around me –
magnetized by change.

Windswept Oaks

These oaks know how to move when
the wind blows strong across the Gulf.
They do not shrink back, do not hesitate,
do not resist like people do. No!
They go gladly with the wind.
The wind sweeps the many trees together.
With wisdom they yield – trunks, branches, crowns –
knitted into one perfect organism,
bending together with grace.
No energy is wasted trying to be upright and singular.
One organism moving with ease
into each perfect wind-blown day.

Fragrance of Kindness

1.

In these days, we hold
the world with great tenderness.
Infinite buddhas encircle us.
The fragrance of kindness is
sweet in the center.
Fierce winds
blow it everywhere.

2.

Long ago, in the Country of Youth,
you took me to the circus.
You gave me some happiness when I was sad.
Now, in China, you walk two hours every day,
backpack loaded with dog food, feeding
homeless dogs half the world away.
Kindness is your way.

Spring Arrived

Spring arrived this year while I was looking east.
I barely noticed. I found no joy
in the tender leaves and colored blossoms.
My heart was full of disbelief.

Now the war has begun.
I look into my heart. Disbelief
has turned to grim acceptance
but I do not give up on peace.
I go out to the garden and pull weeds with new resolve.
I will not turn my back on another spring.

Patch of Grass

Bright winter afternoon, I lie down
on a patch of grass, like the deer often do,
to warm myself in the sun.
The wind is loud and brisk.
Below me, the creek is flowing.
Some songbirds perch on a bare branch nearby.

I am enjoying the scene when it happens.
Did someone turn off the switch?
Without warning, I am just another clump of grass,
a patch of emptiness in the morning sun.
The birds are just birds on a bare branch.
The blue sky – just a blue sky,
the tree – a tree.
The wind empty.

Then the grasping in me
recreates a separate self
with its story about enjoying
the birdsong, the blue sky
and the perfect day – maybe
writing a poem about it later.
I open my eyes…

the birds fly away.

Last Sunset

Today's sun went down quietly through sparse clouds.
A dull sunset, I thought, feeling disappointment.
Moments later the sky is filled
with pink and orange clouds from east to west,
suffused with light from another world.

One moment everything looks still and pale
and the next – intense, golden, billowy light
has sucked the known world into itself
and there is a moment of complete aliveness.

The old terra-cotta roof tiles glow like red coals.
The stone walls are radiant orange.
The few remaining leaves on the poplars
are luminous lanterns sparkling
against the strangely dark blue sky.

I stop, amazed! Everything is so vibrant
and alive inside this intimate moment.
Look! This is how things are.
A moment later the light and color are gone.
The sun of understanding casts itself on the world
and for a moment the possible shines through.

The Necessity that Calls Me

Again and again, the mountain
calls me back as the sun begins to set.
During the day I think it is a lovely mountain.
As the light softens, something stirs inside me
until I can't resist.
Then I follow the footpath
through the aspen trees,
to the top of the little hill
and I bow down obediently –
bow down to the necessity
that calls me.

This World Is Enough

Rain Lilies

Here you are again, your white star body
lifting up from earth on a thin, green thread,
offering yourself to the blue sky.
With no leaves to support you,
you come and go quickly.
When conditions are ripe,
you suddenly appear.
When conditions are not ripe,
you quickly disappear –
forever hiding and seeking.

Robins

1.

The robins are back
with their yellow beaks,
black caps and red breasts.
I saw them on my walk this morning,
hopping along the ground
and into the low juniper branches.
A community of song –
their gleeful sounds
stop the doom, the pall of war,
at least for now.

2.

This morning
first robin arrives
before the sun.

Perched on a bare rose branch
she sings pure notes,
red breast quivering.

Her song in my ear,
my ear inside the morning breeze.
Like this the sun wakes up!

Branches

This morning I lie in bed for a long time –
doing nothing the world can measure –
just looking out the big picture window
at bare branches tossing back and forth
in the morning breeze.

Their long slender arms and fingers, naked and empty,
extend themselves out to a world
neither vertical nor horizontal.

These who have given their bright red jewels –
the best they had to give –
more than one hundred times
and without thought of holding on,
are windblown and wrapped in truth.

Now and then gulls float
in and out of the picture window,
adding and subtracting what they have to give.

I sense what I have to give is my deepest listening –
opening the doors and windows
of my house to all that is,
surrendering to that beauty
completely.

If this were the only world it would be enough.

Spring Shoots

Winter's Back Door

Spring comes in winter's back door
while no one is looking.
Spring arrives full of grace
and extravagance.

First Spider Wart

You push up through winter's wall
trusting life, willing to risk everything –
arrive exactly between two fallen logs,
your long, slender leaves delighted,
poised in a downward arc,
your purple prize riding atop the green stem of you.
You are the beginning and end of life –
a bell waking me up.

Mountain Laurel

You grow near the top of the hill
flocked in lilac-colored buds,
scent still hidden inside the
quietness of your arriving.
I bow my head, gathering near.
A faint fragrance releases itself
to my open senses.

Rusty Black Haw

Innocent of any thought but life,
you produce masses of soft tender leaves,
making way for clusters of tiny flowers
sailing atop the tips of branches,
blown by March breezes.

New Grasses

Green grasses rise up to greet
my crazed and grateful eyes.
I can never feast enough
when brown turns green.

First Buttercup

Here you are - a yellow pool
among the new, green grasses.
Seeing you butters my bread.
Each bite is now!

Lantana

Your vining profusion spreads wildy
across the upper meadow.
Lilac-colored clusters with yellow wombs
shine in the sunlight –
your bounty from winter rains.

Cedar Elm

Your old wound folds in like the mouth
of an ancient woman, teeth gone,
still savoring life, lips rolled inward,
kissing what no longer exists.
Your branches above are
flowering, flowering everywhere.

Your tall trunk is spiked with thin, stubby branches
in the lower realms, close to the earth,
whiskered like the chin of a very old man.
Life still surges inside these veins –
flowering, flowering everywhere.

Field of Bluebonnets

After days of precious rain, the sun pours liquid gold
all over everything. Now is the best time
to fall down gently into the nearest meadow.
Surrender yourself to the grasses and flowers –
to their colors and smells, their stems and leaves,
and the countless creatures with their tiny heartbeats
that keep the world alive.

Fall down quietly into this field of life.
It is your life that you have resisted far too long.
Now your will quivers and gives in.
Your knees and ankles – supple and willing –
dissolve and you become all foot
resting on spongy earth.

Sink down through the leaves and stems,
through the thicket of delicate grasses
and what they call weeds.
Sink down and down into the roots
and nestle there protected
from despair and yearning.
Lie on your back – arms and legs surrendering –
body heavy with giving over to beauty.

Through the thicket of green you will see the sky.
Blue – the color of robins' eggs – and it will be
more blue because the grasses are so green.
The flowers will rise up around you –
bluebonnets, paintbrushes, and primroses.
Their perfume will drift into your pores.
You will see the world as it is.
When you rise up, refreshed,
the meadow will rise up with you
with all its countless beings,
and you will know that you
have never been alone.

High Tide

I sit lodged between two masses of granite
breathing the wet and salty air. My only purpose –
listening to the tide come in – my body sloped
into the cool rock, ears already receiving the water
as it flows into the narrow gorge below.
Tide comes in – all foam and spume and pound –
the guttural laughter of waves
as they finger, fan, and crash against the rocks.

For now, I live inside the sound of water
rolling into a granite tunnel –
curving, purling and slapping against the rock,
sloshing, frothing, lapping eagerly,
then flushing back out quietly
in treasured trickles, gurgles, and gentle flows.
The rush and flush sliding into each other
mingling tempos – one passionate, insistent
the other, grateful and yielding.
I hang here, fastened barnacle-tight,
content with life.

A small and irrelevant loneliness
flickers and falls on my skin
along with misty breath of gray-green sea.
Loneliness, too, is part of the day,
part of this breathing hour.

The Night's Meaning

When I was young,
I always brushed my teeth
to the rhythmic sounds of crickets.
We gave up that freedom when we closed the windows.
Here, worlds away, in this little cabin –
only a screen between me
and the silky night –
I lean over the sink,
brushing and listening, as I used to do,
to the night sing its meaning.

Grasshopper

As the day warms, you open your wings
and fly, thoughtless as wind and wildly into the air,
your yellow torso gleaming in and out of greens and browns.
'Time to live now while the day is ours,'
your clicking castanets proclaim as you
zigzag with zest among wild rose bushes
and plump, still ripening raspberries.
Heat falls off your wings as you dance your delight
into the last days of summer, gladdening the air,
gladdening my heart.

Vertebrae

Dusk comes with no breeze.
I enter the dark pocket of night,
stretch my spent body the length of sun-baked planks,
sinking heavy into some distant forest.
Spine climbs up the memory of lofty sky
nestled among my kin.

Now, as then, round, yellow moon
comes to the standing trees,
splaying light through
masses of leaves,
casting herself soundlessly
onto wooden planks
to linger there.

These wooden planks
feel alive beneath my spine,
reassuring against my tired body –
vertebrae stacked tight
as the still night air.

When I stand up
the ancient forest stands with me
here, beneath the round, yellow moon.

Blades of Grass

Lying here amongst the lazy
blades of grass and idle
wild flowers, life is sweet.
For a lingering moment
no thought of war.

Wading in Bear Lake

What pleasure I get sloshing back and forth
in the delicious, cold and sandy shallows
of this glacial-fed lake.

My ears like the sounds of sloshing.
My feet enjoy the touch of small pebbles pushing
into heels and balls – left foot, right foot.

Two ducks paddle in and out of the cove,
looking toward me in silent greeting.
They scratch and preen, then dive down,
tails and webbed feet straight up in the air.
Maybe they are looking at my feet.

A yellow fish with black speckles swims
near my feet, nips the water, then continues on,
nearly missing the duck.
No bother!

Like the ducks, my feet are more comfortable
in the water, content to slosh back and forth,
living these golden days with ease.

Watermelon

The essential summer –

Cobalt blue bowl with its white flowers
holds this juicy, red, red watermelon
with its shiny black, black seeds just until

the hinge of my mouth opens wide.
Then cold, sweet melon slides
down the dark passage of my throat
and into its next becoming.

Tree Offering

You give your shadow to the sun to do with as it will.
The sun takes it and throws it against
the stucco wall where it temporarily abides.

I come along just as this marvelous gift is offered –
tree blazing with winter light,
it's shadow self nearby.
The kind of light that burns
a simple happiness into the mind.

Hillside Theater

Even though the world is suffering –
and this suffering belongs to us –
at dusk, we walk quietly through the meadow,
through the aspen grove and up the hillside
to sit among the yellow and white flowers,
to sit attentively facing the mountain
just before the door of darkness closes on this day.

Clouds gather in the west
and quiet settles across the mountain
and in our bones.

The sun takes its final bow
and melts down into the rock.
Then, like a child who doesn't want to sleep,
it peeks upward just before the chill.

Mountain settles into itself, unperturbed,
darkens even as the sky turns
rose and orange – sliver of blue, deep gray.

We settle and settle into the hillside,
enfolded in darkness, wrapped
in the implicate order of all things.
We sit in stillness as the mountain does.

A few dozen blackbirds imprint the sky
between us and the mountain
as they return to their forest.
My heart leaps up as I see them
pass before me, dreamlike and strange –
a transit I can only imagine.

But we have our own transit.
Tonight's guide all the way home,
the rose-petal moon.

Old Barn

Slowly, over time
the barn – aged and goose-kneed –
fell down in a full bow.
Down and down into the wild grasses,
gently it fell and slowly
into the wild grasses.
Ribs burdened with heavy snows
year after year, finally let go,
let fate fall, fall into the wild grasses
and there it settled with
a deep satisfied sigh!

While the barn was falling,
cars were driving by
with long floppy-eared dogs
hanging out the windows,
faces curved and smiling into the wind,
gulping air, filled with raw happiness.

The barn settled down and down –
its underbelly tickled by wild grasses.
The breeze blew across the top of it
and it continued to be.

Migrations

Guests come to the land tonight.
I hear their thick, throaty calls.
Hear them gathering and surrounding the stone house
like other times back East
when Canadian geese took refuge
at a friend's farm on their way south for winter.
I can still feel the crisp, stone-cold air
on my cheeks as I went out to meet their honks.

These friends are unknown to me.
Their sounds are strange and unfamiliar
almost lusty, perhaps hungry for the refuge this land provides.
I go out to greet them on a warm, breezy night,
yellow moon ripening.

You are welcome here, dear friends,
for a night or for the winter.
Talk your strange talk and fill me with your difference.
Stay awhile if you have no place to be.
We will tell each other stories of our people
and sing each other songs of our survival.

Mind of Love

Walking Stick

How you got inside
the plastic light box
I don't know.

Your long, thin, stick body
lay perfectly straight,
belly-side up,

all six legs folded neatly
and crossed over your torso.
As though you meant to die

and die with dignity.
As though you meant to
lie down in this sarcophagus

on the hard bed of faith,
resolved to leave the body –
now a peaceful, empty shell.

Leave it behind for a place
your walking stick legs
can't take you.

Baby Praying Mantis

Real life just crawled
onto my left hand.
Fresh, light green –

color of new leaves in spring.
Lighter than goose down
she caresses my fingers,

crawls over a knuckle.
Diligent and awake, she crawls,
all six legs, over my wrist,

up the top of my forearm,
crosses into the dark territory
of my black shirt –

her green body even more fresh,
and now up my deltoid,
tracing the pain of so many lifetimes,

she crawls over my shoulder,
up my neck
and into my graying hair.

Real life –
aimless and fresh and now –
awakens the mind of love.

Wasp

The sting of a wasp is unforgettable.
Feeling it once, you will wish to avoid another sting.
You may want to kill all wasps.

Fear of the sting is natural until you learn to trust the wasp,
learn to trust her completely. She knows when to sting.

When she offers you her sting, take heart!
She is giving you the right medicine.
Something changes inside
and you begin to heal other wounds,
older than water.

When her time is up, she falls to the ground
in a soundless boom. You will find her there
when you sweep the floor, wings and body stiff.

If you are there when she falls –
if you squint your eyes
and expect nothing –
you might see
                her soul
                          fly

                                        away –

Then you will know your fear was useless, even extravagant.
When it's your turn to die you'll fall to the ground
in a soundless boom.

Then quietly rise up *and fly!*

Bird Being

I was driving a little too fast.
You were flying low, enjoying your life.
Suddenly, I heard your little body as it hit,
then bounced off my car.
The dull sound flew into my body.
In the rearview mirror, I saw you bounce exactly twice
and land in the middle of the road.

I turned back, back towards your
helplessness, towards life's frailty –
towards the slender question
of where you end and I begin.

Holding you now, I feel your
small heart slowing down, and down.
Your wings have stopped flapping. I
stroke your breast so gently, whispering
"I'm sorry." Even as your wings and legs
become rigid, your breast feels so alive.
Your quivering breast is the last to speak
with its soft yielding, offering no blame, no clinging.

I will never forget the feeling of life bleeding away
from the form of you as the great timekeeper paused,
and we stood together on the side of the road.

Sky of Mind

The massive dome of pink granite
lifts off the ground in a grand gesture,
taking few trees with it as it climbs
to its smooth, flat summit near the clouds.

Some nights, the clouds dip down and swim
in little pools that lie scattered about.
Clouds enjoy the game of being everywhere at once.
When the moon comes out,
she catches the fun,
and without any effort,
there's a moon in every pool.

Up here on the summit,
surrounded by boundless clouds and moons,
and hundreds of billions of stars,
the mind is free to be
everywhere at once,
shining, shining.

Blooming Beyond Death

They say you died last month
but I see you clearly in the iris bulbs
you gave me years ago, dug from your garden –
a cycle complete.

I remember you best in the sunbonnet you made
of scraps of cloth from an old housedress.
You are bending over the peas and beans, tomatoes and okra
tenderly and patiently weeding, watering, harvesting.
I remember your flower garden – purple and white iris.
You could make them bloom longer than anyone.

I see you just as clearly this morning in the white iris
blooming with ease in my garden for the first time
after six years of dormancy,
swaying in the light morning breeze.
I can feel your happiness and your freedom, leaving
the old body behind with all its pain and limitation –
for the jewels of true freedom –
free to bloom when and where you choose.

Compassion

Following my breath here in the darkness,
body invisible, I feel more animal than human.
The sound of coyote howling is familiar and comforting,
while the sound of the refrigerator motor is alien to me.
When it clicks off, an edginess subsides.

Inside the stone house on this chilly night,
my eyes hone down on nothing.
I can hear my animal heart beating and feel kinship
with all that lives beyond these walls.

Taking another breath of fragrant life
I ride deep into the night –
beyond walls or need for walls.
Out there where coyote howls
and stars peer down through eons of darkness
with eyes of compassion.

Hammock

This body makes no effort –
hangs motionless for a long time
as wind rocks it back and forth.
All around us, night sounds –
screech owl, cricket, wind chime,
leaves tickling together,
bugs crawling in the dead leaves.
Delight! Listening, to each single sound
flowing into the great emptiness,
great cavity of night.
No singular thing in this abyss of hope.
Body surrendering, mind letting go,
fathoming unity, as each sound
surrenders its note to the one true song.

Happiness

Joy comes visiting
more easily now –
lingers

quietly on my lips,
unfurling a smile
long hidden

among the soft
mosses of confusion
and self-doubt.

Such happiness
beneath the pale green
mosses, patiently waiting.

I am coming home,
home to myself.
Joyful and trusting,

steps solid and free,
I am returning home to myself,
bright with seeing.

Big Sky

I step outside at dusk,
leaving the walls and roof behind.
Lost in thought.

Before I know it, whoosh –
big sky rises up to meet me,
much bigger than I remember.

With quiet strength, big sky pulls me into itself.
Big sky at dusk with its white, feathery clouds
and emptiness everywhere pulls me away
from the world of things.

Night Blooming Cereus

By what miracle of dark devotion
do you arise from your thorny past
to give yourself away?

By what sheer will for beauty
do you pose your petals,
round and bulbous, to the stars
who signal their approval
even though silent?

By what magnitude of trust
do you dare to open the soft
flesh of your quivering arms
in a hostile world?

By what nostalgia for perfection
does such sweet perfume slip quietly
from your innermost shrine
into the poisonous air,
the pure fragrance that offers
a revolution, here and now?

By what holy madness
do you dare
to dream
of change?

About the Author

Paméla Overeynder lives in Austin, Texas. She spends her free time outdoors — these days in the Barton Creek Greenbelt near her home where she practices living in the present moment. Her poetry, an expression of the moments of living presence, explores the intimacies of nature and inquires into the apparent boundaries between the human form, the natural world and the vastness beyond. She has published in **Borderlands Texas Poetry Review** and **The Mindfullness Bell,** an international Buddhist journal. She is currently working on a new book of poems.

www.ingramcontent.com/pod-product-compliance
Lightning Source LLC
Chambersburg PA
CBHW071029080526
44587CB00015B/2547